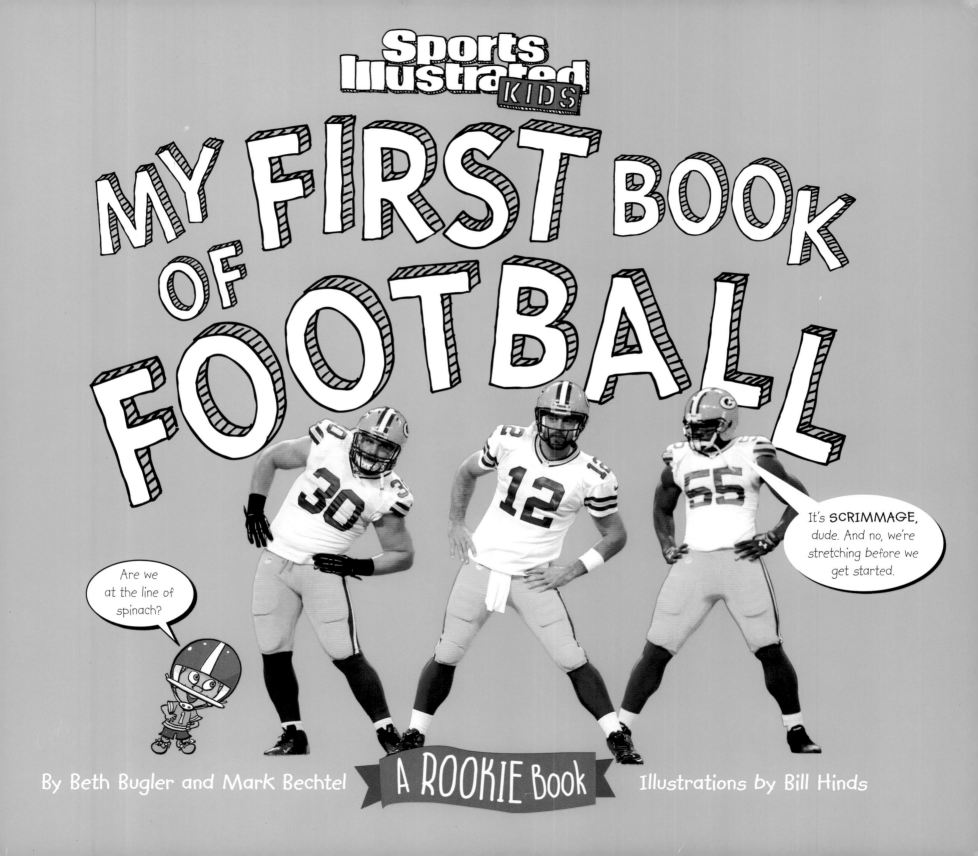

Football is an action-packed game played by

TWO TEAMS

of (mostly) big guys who try to score
as many points as possible.

Each team has

11 PLAYERS

on the field at a time.

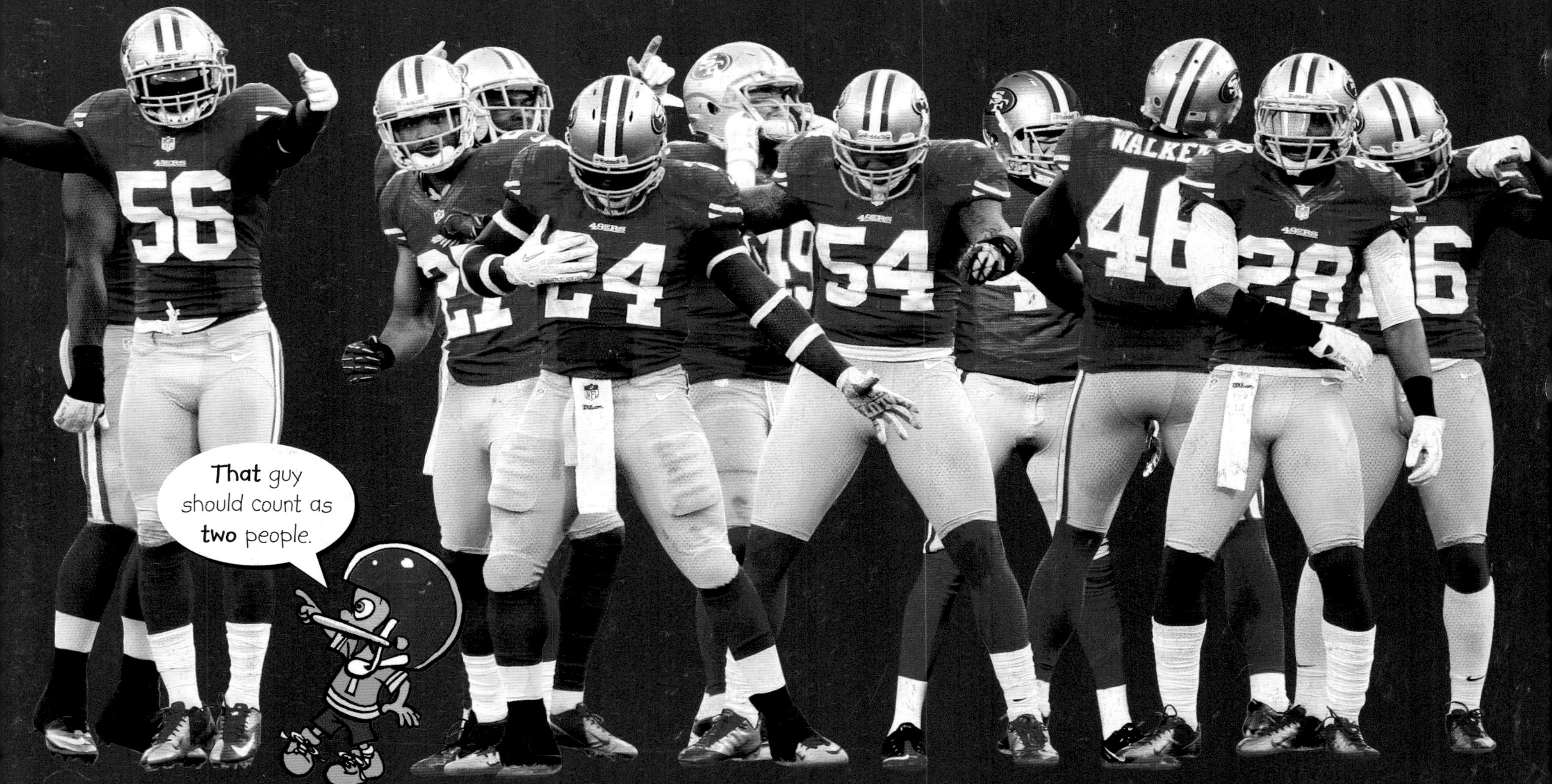

The game is divided into

FOUR QUARTERS

that are **15 MINUTES** each.

1   2   3   4

Here, after the second quarter, comes

HALFTIME.

That's a short break
for everyone!

A break?
But we're just
getting started!

The **FIELD** is **100 YARDS** long.

That's like **8** school buses in a row!

The two teams take turns trying to move the ball into the **END ZONE.**

This is where players score and the points add up!

And where I bust out my **end zone dance!!**

To determine which team gets the ball first, the captains and the officials get together for a friendly, old-school

COIN TOSS.

The captain of the visiting team gets to call "heads" or "tails." Whoever wins the toss gets to decide if they want the ball.

Excuse me, I'll need that **QUARTER** back.

...KICKOFF!

The kicker boots the ball down the field.

So THAT'S why they call it football.

A player from the other team catches the ball and runs with it toward the end zone until . . .

I got it!
I got it!
I **DON'T** got it!

. . . he gets

TACKLED!

Oof! That means he's
brought to the ground
by an opponent.

TIMBER!!

TIME

14:47

Please let me land on something soft. Please let me land on something soft. Please let me land on something soft . . . .

Now the two teams each gather in a

HUDDLE

to go over their strategy.

This is the

COACH.

→

He tells the guys which plays to run.

This is the

QUARTERBACK.

He's the big cheese, the main man who calls the shots on the field when his team has the ball.

Did I forget to lock the house this morning?

The players with the ball are called the

OFFENSE.

TIME
8:45

The guys who are trying to stop them are the

DEFENSE.

Can we get this show on the road? My back is **killing** me!

The coach calls a running play.

The QB will

HAND OFF

the ball to a running back, who takes off down the field.

QUARTER
2ND

The offense has four chances, called DOW

TIME

15:00

NS, to move the ball **10 YARDS.** If they do, they get to keep the ball.

Give me the ball! I'm almost there!

Sorry, pal. You only got eight yards. That means it's **second down,** and you need two more yards.

For this play, the quarterback will

PASS

the ball to a receiver, who tries to catch it.

Launch it!

QUARTER
2ND

Caught it! And he got
enough yards for a

FIRST DOWN!

The offense gets to keep driving
the football toward the end zone.

This way?

But if the offense gets stuck and it's

FOURTH DOWN,

they have a **big** decision to make. If they run or pass and don't make a first down, they lose the ball.

However, if they are close enough to the end zone, they can try a

FIELD GOAL.

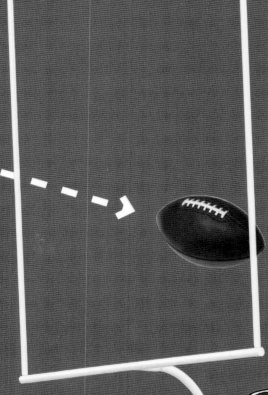

The kicker sends the ball through the goalposts—his team gets three points!

Look at the clock! It's almost time for that *break*, right?

HALFT

O.K., everyone!
While the coaches talk
to the players in the
locker room, it's your
chance to take care of:

1.

Getting a snack.

IME!!!

2. Stretching your legs.

3. Whatever else needs to be taken care of.

QUARTER

3RD

At the beginning of the

SECOND HALF,

the team that got the ball to start the game kicks off.

Oops!
The QB missed his receiver.
It's an

INCOMPLETE PASS.

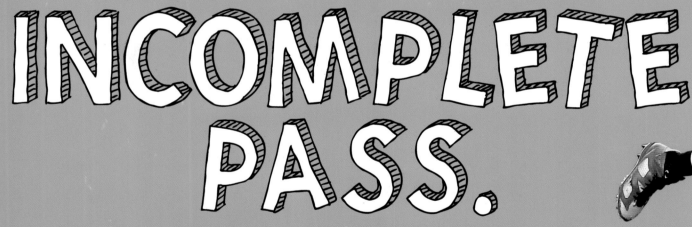

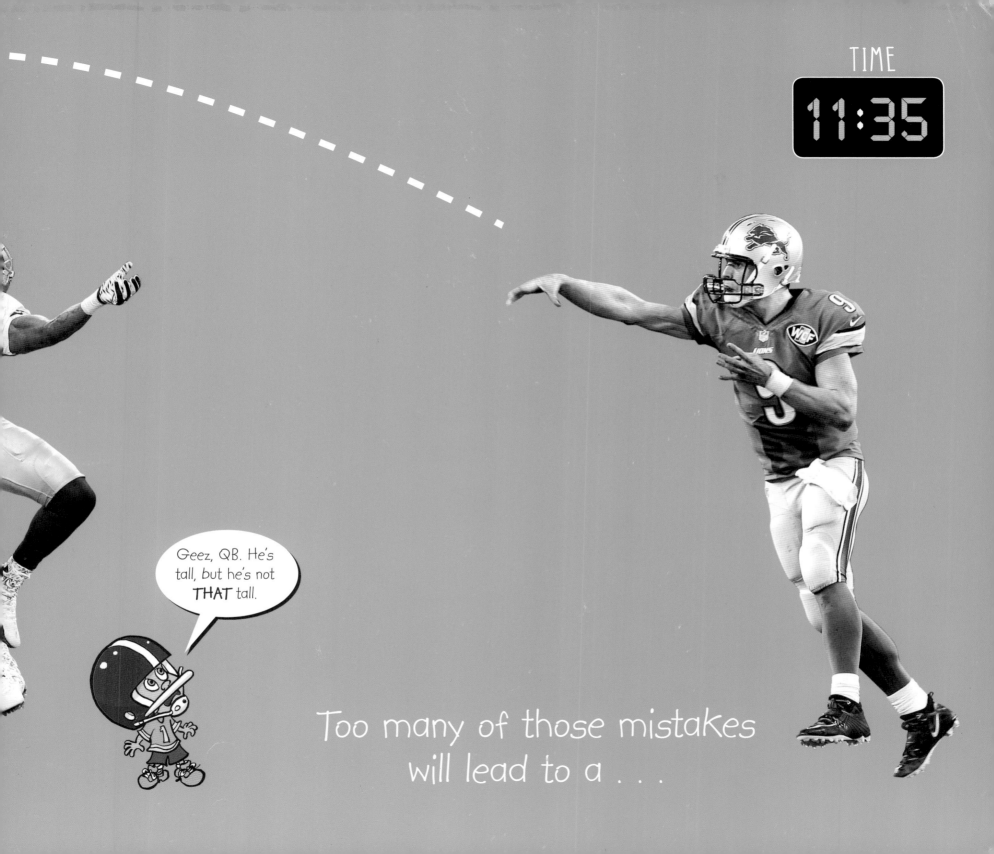

The offense isn't close enough to try for a field goal, so they decide to

PUNT.

The punter kicks the ball down the field, giving the ball to the other team.

Wow! You're flexible, but can you do this?

But wait. What's that

FLAG

on the field? An official threw it there because someone broke a rule and committed a

PENALTY.

The guilty team is punished. If it's the defense, the ball is moved closer to the end zone. If it's the offense, the ball is moved farther away.

And no video games for a week!

Ha! Got it!

D'oh! That was mine!

The quarterback is trying to complete another pass. Yikes! It's an

INTERCEPTION!

A player for the other team caught the ball.

Time is running out!
The fourth quarter is almost
over. The quarterback
throws the ball to an
open receiver.

He catches it, and
he's heading toward
the end zone.

It's a

UCHDOWN!

He made it into the end zone.
That's six points! And his team will get
a chance to score one more point if they
kick the ball through the goalposts!

But first . . . .

End zone dance!

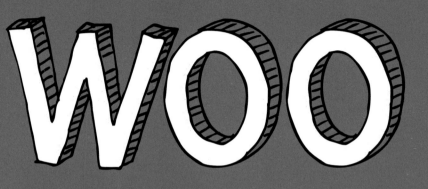

WOO HOO!

I don't know what you call that move, but I call this **The Shake with a Small Fry!**

The clock hits zero.

GAME OVER!

It's time to celebrate!

That was **awesome!** I can't wait to do it again. But next time I'm bringing my umbrella!

TIME INC. BOOKS

Publisher Margot Schupf
Vice President, Finance Vandana Patel
Executive Director, Marketing Services Carol Pittard
Executive Director, Business Development Suzanne Albert
Executive Director, Marketing Susan Hettleman
Executive Publishing Director Megan Pearlman
Associate Director of Publicity Courtney Greenhalgh
Assistant General Counsel Simone Procas
Assistant Director, Special Sales Ilene Schreider
Assistant Director, Finance Christine Font
Assistant Production Director Susan Chodakiewicz
Senior Manager, Sales Marketing Danielle Costa
Senior Manager, Children's Category Marketing Amanda Lipnick
Associate Prepress Manager Alex Voznesenskiy
Associate Project Manager Stephanie Braga

Editorial Director Stephen Koepp
Art Director Gary Stewart
Senior Editors Roe D'Angelo, Alyssa Smith
Managing Editor Matt DeMazza
Editor, Children's Books Jonathan White
Copy Chief Rina Bander
Design Manager Anne-Michelle Gallero
Assistant Managing Editor Gina Scauzillo
Editorial Assistant Courtney Mifsud

Special thanks: Allyson Angle, Katherine Barnet, Brad Beatson, Jeremy Biloon, Ian Chin, Rose Cirrincione, Pat Datta, Assu Etsubneh, Alison Foster, Erika Hawxhurst, Kristina Jutzi, David Kahn, Jean Kennedy, Hillary Leary, Samantha Long, Amy Mangus, Kimberly Marshall, Robert Martells, Nina Mistry, Melissa Presti, Danielle Prielipp, Kate Roncinske, Babette Ross, Dave Rozzelle, Matthew Ryan, Ricardo Santiago, Divyam Shrivastava

ISBN 10: 1-61893-151-2
ISBN 13: 978-1-61893-151-1
Library of Congress Control Number: 2015935761

Sports Illustrated Kids is a trademark of Time Inc.

We welcome your comments and suggestions about Sports Illustrated Kids Books. Please write to us at:
Sports Illustrated Kids Books
Attention: Book Editors
P.O. Box 361095
Des Moines, IA 50336-1095

If you would like to order any of our hardcover Collector's Edition books, please call us at 800-327-6388 (Monday through Friday, 7 a.m.–9 p.m. Central Time).

1 TLF 15